The Complete Guide to Astrology

Explore Every Astrology of Different Religions

By

Teresa Muller

SPECIAL DISCLAIMER

All the information's included in this book are given for instructive, informational and entertainment purposes, the author can claim to share very good quality recipes but is not headed for the perfect data and uses of the mentioned recipes, in fact the information's are not intent to provide dietary advice without a medical consultancy.

The author does not hold any responsibility for errors, omissions or contrary interpretation of the content in this book.

It is recommended to consult a medical practitioner before to approach any kind of diet, especially if you have a particular health situation, the author isn't headed for the responsibility of these situations and everything is under the responsibility of the reader, the author strongly recommend to preserve the health taking all precautions to ensure ingredients are fully cooked.

Table of Contents

Introduction to Astrology

Astrology is a pseudoscience that professes to divine data about social issues and earthbound occasions by examining the developments and relative places of heavenly articles.

Astrology has been dated to in any event the second thousand years BCE. It has its underlying foundations in calendrical frameworks used to foresee regular movements and to decipher heavenly cycles as indications of awesome interchanges.

Numerous societies have connected significance to galactic occasions, and a few, for example, the Hindus, Chinese, and the Maya— created expound frameworks for foreseeing natural occurrences from heavenly perceptions. Western astrology, one of the most established prophetic structures still being used, can follow its foundations to the nineteenth seventeenth century BCE Mesopotamia, from which it spread to Ancient Greece, Rome, the Arab world, and in the long run Central and Western Europe.

Contemporary Western astrology is frequently connected with frameworks of horoscopes that indicate to clarify parts of an individual's character and anticipate noteworthy occasions in their lives dependent on the places of heavenly articles; most of expert crystal gazers depend on such frameworks.

All through the more significant part of its history, astrology was viewed as an insightful convention. It was essential in scholarly circles, regularly in close connection with stargazing, speculative chemistry, meteorology, and medication. It was available in political circles and is referenced in different works of writing, from Dante Alighieri and Geoffrey Chaucer to William Shakespeare, Lope de Vega, and Calderón de la Barca.

Following the finish of the nineteenth century and the wide-scale appropriation of the logical technique, astrology has been tested adequately on both theoretical and trial grounds. It has been appeared to have no rational legitimacy or illustrative force. Astrology accordingly lost its academic and hypothetical standing, and strong faith in it has, to a great extent, declined. While surveys have shown that roughly one-fourth of American, British, and Canadian individuals state they keep on accepting that star and planet positions influence their lives, astrology is currently perceived as a pseudoscience—a conviction that is inaccurately introduced as logical.

Astrology mixes science and instinct, magic and math, cycles, and also signs. It focuses on planets, and even their periods, as well as asteroids, are actual. They're so real that their motions are consistent and also recordable. Astrology permits us to draw parallels between the orbits of heavenly bodies and even events down right here in the world. It enables us to browse the planetary waves by eying our very own "tidal tables," or global ephemerides, and also by figuring out exactly how to get the most effective trip from the tide that's en route. It validates our suspicions as well as supports what we currently understand. Astrology is a language, an icon set, and also a guide to recognizing the globe, life, and also the Cosmos.

Your astrology graph or your horoscope is your map, computed utilizing the date and time you were born from the viewpoint of your birth location.

From that details, a circular, clock-shaped layout arises that programs where every Earth, star as well as the Planet was located at the moment you create/make your debut.

Your chart is a traditional cosmic snapshot that freeze-frames deep space specifically as it was from your viewpoint. You carry that very same point of view around with you throughout life. The horoscope chart is your plan-- your planetary knapsack, a proprietor's manual that shows what you packed into your "tool-kit" for this lifetime and also precisely how best to use it. Everyone's got one, and also no two are ever before the very same, which is rather fantastic. However, there's more-- given that the graph is a map, everybody's got one of whatever.

Professional astrologers do not hold with their traditional theories of holy impact. Instead, the modern astrologist visualizes the heavens and Earth as joined, interpenetrating, as well as sharing a standard room and also time. The wonderful planetary or holy occasions occurring around and even past the Planet (eclipses, lineups, and more) are not seen as CAUSING incidents globally. Still, as fantastic trademarks of events ALSO happening below on Earth. In simple words, there is no specific reason in the heavens complied with by a "result" below on Earth. Instead, both planetary and earthly occasions occur all at once and also are mutually reflective. Neither is the reason for the various other; both are the item of the minute, one acted out in the paradises over, the various other below on the Planet below.

In recap, astrology is the research of delicate cycles and planetary occasions as they are reflected in our earthly atmosphere and also vice- versa-- a large cosmic clock. Astrologists locate the planetary patterns revealed in the rhythmic motions of the Earth fantastic assistance in light on the seeming helter-skelter of day-to-day life. Astrologists may have their heads in the heavens, however, just to far better overview their feet right here on Earth.

Astrodomes horoscopes are understandable, even for those that have not taken care of astrology before - you need not understand any one of the clinical jargons entailed to be able to profit from our horoscope readings. If we are lucky, however, your passion for this fascinating subject matter has been stirred up by one of our brief texts. This short online intro can help make you familiar with a lot of the astrological techniques and provide you a standard understanding of how it's all done.

If you want to learn more regarding astrology, we recommend you read a few of the standard textbooks mentioned in our bibliography or call an astrology college near you. Astrology sees humanity as being not just influenced by genetic variables and also the environment, however, likewise by the state of our solar system at the moment of birth. The Earth is considered fundamental life-forces, the tools we obey along with the basis of our very substance. These secular forces tackle various types, depending upon their zodiacal position and how they relate to each other.

Solar-System: The facets created in between the Earth define these relationships. The placements of the worlds about the place of birth inform us of their expression in the balls of life illustrated by the astrological houses.

By analyzing the duties of these gamers (the planets) and also their top qualities (the aspects, signs, and even homes) and also developing a synthesis, astrology can provide a full and detailed picture of the individual and also his possibility, based on the natal horoscope.

Since Halloween, something ominous has been occurring in the heavens. Something that is presumably a factor in the present descent right into the mayhem that everybody's lives seem to have been taking.

No, it isn't a winter climate advisory, nor is it the slow-moving, however distressing method of finals. Mercury remains in retrograde, as well as for every person that seems like their life has become an out-of-control dumpster fire, there might be a factor for it that's much less related to midterms and also more about the stars.

For those who are unaware of astrology, the method involves reading and also analyzing the placement of celestial objects and exactly how they affect social events. This is usually done via checking out an individual's natal graph, which is a snapshot of the astrological skies at the precise minute of birth. The placement of the Sunlight, Moon, worlds, and comets all affect an individual's birth chart, and the energy they stand for can be materialized in a wide range of methods conjunction with where the heavenly bodies are.

It is essential to acknowledge that astrology is taken into consideration a kind of pseudoscience by the clinical and also academia's and lots of do not see it as an accurate or reliable means to evaluate info due to the untestable nature of the cases as well as unbacked research study. Though it may not be a clinically approved practice, the history and the art type can be used either as a fun event method, or a curiosity sustained hobby.

The very best analogy I have generated to explain the astrological schedule and its' numerous ins and outs is by comparing it to a pizza. The 12 indicators, Aries, Taurus, Gemini, etc., resemble the crust, acting as a turning-around structure of the holy range in which all various other stellar occasions occur. The signs are the standard of an individual's character and identity, hence impacting the temperament of a particular principle.

The calendar is then broken down into 12 houses, which are interpreted to rule over different elements of life like marital relationship, creativity, and also financial resources. Your homes stay in the location, relative to the indications, and each section can be broken down by various subtleties relying on the degree juxtaposed to the indicator. They are like the sauce as well as cheese. Houses function as the fundamental atmosphere for results in life along with specs for characteristics. Lastly, the Earth is like the garnishes, which suggest the certain subtleties of a person's identity. Each world and astrological body policies, a particular trait like communication, Love, and hostility, which directly connects with your house and indication that the Planet remains in.

These predetermined attributes can be manifested in an individual's life in a wide variety of ways depending on which zodiac constellation Earth remains in and which house it drops under— hence producing the chance for limitless results and features. As the celestial bodies relocate, they are believed to influence whatever parts of life that they rule.

So, when Mercury, the planet of communication, modern technology, and travel, appears to move backward in the sky, it creates a significant amount of concerns in locations of life concerning travel, technology, and interaction. Computers and also phones are known to quit working, organizing problems arise, as well as everybody becomes just a little bit even worse at connecting their thoughts as well as sensations. This repeating chaotic event is called retrograde, and it occurs about three times a year for Mercury.

An individual can identify their most likely job choices, sex life, interaction design, and past youth trauma from their birth graph relying on where particular worlds lie along with your homes, indicators, and each other. All one needs to see their chart is their date of birth, time of delivery, and also the city of birth. Plug the details into a natal graph calculator, and it'll be generated in addition to a description of each positioning.

There are many misunderstandings concerning astrology. For instance, the horoscopes listed in the day-to-day papers are just based upon the indicator placement of the Sunlight. In contrast, full natal astrology takes many more things right into account. The application of astrology to individuals can become close to as a research of originality, from either an emotional perspective or on an anticipating, event-based level.

The main principles to understand in astrology are the Planets, Indicators, Houses, and also the connections in between them, which are called Aspects. From an astrological viewpoint, each person's unique originality is based on the endless variants of these four elements. Astrology is a scientific research study of innovation, and the astrological graph offers a particular photo of the unique means each person is "wired." In fact, because of the varying rate of each world's orbit around the Sunlight, an individual's birth chart is not copied for greater than 25,000 years!

The energies that were active in the ambiance at the precise minute of your birth were stamped on the cellular level of your extremely being and remain a part of you throughout this lifetime. Your birth chart is a schematic: a graph that reveals this "internal wiring" you were born with, yet what you do with that electrical wiring depends on you.

Astrology is a tool to obtain an objective understanding of your patterns of actions. Most of us have propensities that lead to inappropriate effects and sensations of isolation and also misery. The method is to uncover our own "problems" and also encourage ourselves to prevent them. With this objective understanding, we can choose to make modifications that lead to our life running much more smoothly.

Astrology itself is not spiritual, yet it can be a reliable device for breaking the ice to accessing our spirituality. By understanding our psychological circuitry (as objectively envisioned in the astrology chart), we can approve and deal with ourselves with even more understanding and detachment. This calms the turmoil of the inner character as well as enables our natural spiritual nature to emerge.

And also, by recognizing the psychological electrical wiring of others through their astrological charts, we can much more conveniently accept their distinct distinctions without taking it so directly; we can find out to take pleasure in the range rather than looking for to transform others right into an expansion of ourselves. So although astrology is not spiritual, it can result in critical spiritual experiences, such as unconditional caring approval.

In finding out to utilize astrology in your life, it is vital to get some understanding of the four components of any type of birth chart: The Planets, Signs, Homes, and Aspects. What follows is some basic info you will certainly require to translate and also use your table. Having your chart convenient as you read this information will enable you to start to tune-in to what the mixes of Earth, sign as well as residence seem like in your very own chart, and also this is an excellent means to start to comprehend how astrology functions.

History of astrology

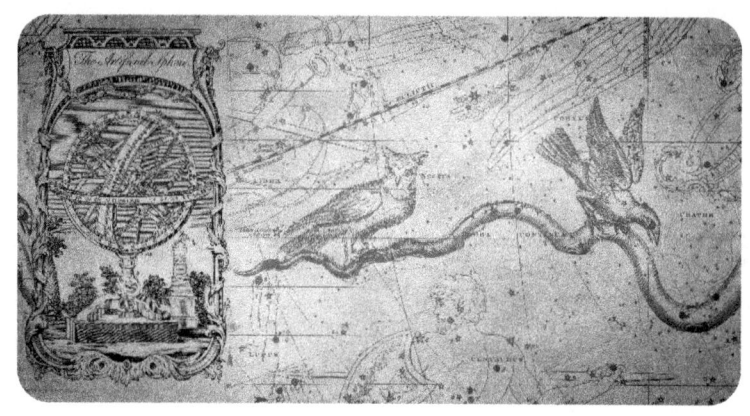

Astrological beliefs in documents between celestial monitoring and also earthbound occasions have affected numerous elements of human history, including worldviews, language as well as multiple components of social culture.

Amongst Indo-European individuals, astrology has been dated to the third millennium BC, with origins in calendrical systems made use of to forecast seasonal changes and to translate holy cycles as signs of excellent communications.

Till the 17th century, astrology was thought about an academic custom, and it assisted drive the development of astronomy. It was generally approved in political as well as social circles, and several of its concepts were utilized in various other traditional studies, such as alchemy, meteorology, and also medicine. By the end of the 17th century, rising scientific concepts in astronomy, such as heliocentrism, weakened the academic basis of astrology, which ultimately shed its scholastic standing and ended up being considered a pseudoscience. Empirical clinical investigation has shown that forecasts and suggestions based on these systems are not precise.

In the 20th century, astrology acquired broader consumer popularity via the influence of regular information media products, such as paper horoscopes.

Astrology, in its broadest feeling, is the look for human definition overhead; it seeks to recognize primary and details social habits with the influence of worlds and various other celestial objects. It has been suggested that astrology started as a study as quickly as humans made conscious efforts to determine, record, as well as forecast seasonal changes by reference to vast cycles.

Very early proof of such methods looks like markings on bones and cave wall surfaces, which reveal that lunar cycles were being kept in mind as very early as 25,000 years ago; the first step in the direction of tape-recording the Moon's impact upon trends as well as rivers, and also in the course of arranging a public calendar. With the Neolithic farming revolution, new demands were additionally fulfilled by raising expertise of constellations, whose looks in the night-time sky modification with the periods, allowing the rising of certain star-groups to herald annual floodings or seasonal activities. By the 3rd millennium BC, prevalent civilizations had developed sophisticated awareness of holy cycles, and also are believed to have knowingly oriented their sacred places to create alignment with the heliacal risings of the celebrities.

There is spread evidence to suggest that the earliest recognized astrological recommendations are copies of messages made throughout this duration, particularly in Mesopotamia (Sumer, Akkad, Assyria, and also Babylonia). 2, from the Venus tablet computer of Ammisaduqa (assembled in Babylon around 1700 BC) are reported to have been made throughout the reign of king Sargon of Akkad (2334-2279 BC). One more, showing a very early use election astrology, is ascribed to the regime of the Sumerian ruler Gudea of Lagash. This describes how the gods revealed to him in a desire the constellations that would be best for the planned building and construction of a holy place. Nonetheless, the debate goes on whether they were genuinely videotaped at the time or just ascribed to old leaders by posterity. The earliest undisputed proof of the use of astrology as an integrated system of understanding is, for that reason, credited to the documents that emerge from the very first empire of Mesopotamia (1950-1651 BC).

Ancient globe

Babylonian astrology was the first organized system of astrology, developing in the 2nd millennium BC. There is speculation that astrology of some kind appeared in the Sumerian duration in the third millennium BC. Yet, the isolated recommendations to old celestial omens dated to this duration are ruled out sufficient evidence to demonstrate an incorporated theory of astrology. The history of scholarly holy prophecy is, for that reason, typically reported beginning with late Old Babylonian messages (c. 1800 BC), proceeding through the Middle Babylonian as well as Middle Assyrian periods (c. 1200 BC).

By the 16th century BC, the considerable employment of omen-based astrology can be confirmed in the compilation of a thorough reference work known as Enuma Anu Enlil. Its materials contained 70 cuneiform tablets making up 7,000 celestial omens. Texts from this time likewise refer to an oral custom - the beginning and web content of which can only be hypothesized upon. Right now, Babylonian astrology was only mundane, worried with the prediction of weather and political matters. Also, before the 7th century BC, the specialists' understanding of astronomy was reasonably straightforward. Astrological icons likely stood for seasonal tasks, as well as we're used as an annual almanac of noted tasks to advise a community to make points appropriate to the period or weather (such as icons standing for times for harvesting, collecting shell-fish, angling by internet or line, sowing crops, accumulating or handling water gets, searching, as well as seasonal jobs crucial in making sure the survival of kids as well as young pets for the larger group). By the fourth century, their mathematical methods had progressed enough to determine future global settings with affordable precision; after that, extensive ephemerides started to appear.

Babylonian astrology developed within the context of prophecy. A collection of 32 tablets with specific liver designs, dating from 1875 BC, are the earliest well-known detailed messages of Babylonian divination, and these demonstrate the very same interpretational style as that used in holy omen evaluation. Blemishes, as well as marks located on the liver of the sacrificial pet, were interpreted as symbolic indications that offered messages from the gods to the king.

The gods were additionally believed to offer themselves in the holy photos of the piles of Earth or celebrities with whom they were connected. Evil celestial prophecies attached to any kind of specific Earth were therefore seen as signs of discontentment or disruption of the God that Planet stood for. Such indications were consulted with efforts to appease God and discover manageable ways through which God's expression could be known without substantial damage to the king and his country. An astronomical report to Esarhaddon concerning a great lunar eclipse of January 673 BC demonstrates how the ritualistic use substitute kings, or replacement occasions, combined an unquestioning belief in magic and omens with a simple mechanical view that the astrological event must have some sort of correlate within the environment:

At first of the year, flooding will undoubtedly come and also damage the dikes. As a substitute for the king, I will undoubtedly puncture a wall, here in Babylonia, in the middle of the night. No one will indeed find out about it.

Ulla Koch-Westenholz, in her 1995 publication Mesopotamian Astrology, says that this ambivalence between atheistic as well as mechanic worldview defines the Babylonian concept of celestial divination as one which, despite its heavy reliance on magic, stays free of ramifications of targeted punishment with the objective of revenge, and so "shares several of the defining attributes of modern-day scientific research: it is objective as well as value-free, it runs according to well-known guidelines, and its information are considered universally valid as well as can be sought out in composed inventories." Koch-Westenholz also establishes the essential difference in between ancient Babylonian astrology and also various other divinatory self-controls as being that the former was initially solely interested in ordinary astrology, being geographically oriented and also mainly applied to countries cities and even nations, and nearly entirely worried about the well-being of the state and the king as the governing head of the country. Mundane astrology is, for that reason, understood to be among the oldest branches of astrology. It was just with the gradual introduction of horoscopic astrology, from the sixth century BC, that astrology created the methods and also a practice of natal astrology.

Hellenistic Egypt

In 525 BC, Egypt was overcome by the Persians, so there is most likely to have been some Mesopotamian influence on Egyptian astrology. Arguing in favor of this, chronicler Tamsyn Barton gives an instance of what seems Mesopotamian influence on the Egyptian Zodiac, which shared two signs-- the Equilibrium and the Scorpion, as confirmed in the Dendera Zodiac (in the Greek variation the Equilibrium was referred to as the Scorpion's Claws).

After the line of work by Alexander the Great in 332 BC, Egypt came under Hellenistic policy and impact. The Alexandria city was founded by Alexander after the occupation, and also during the 3rd and 2nd centuries BC, the scholars of Alexandria were prolific authors. It remained in Ptolemaic Alexandria that Babylonian astrology was blended with the Egyptian tradition of Decanic astrology to develop Horoscopic astrology. This contained the Babylonian zodiac signs and calendar with its system of worldly exaltations, the triplicities of the indicators, and also the significance of eclipses.

Together with this, it integrated the Egyptian principle of dividing the Zodiac right into thirty-six decans of ten levels each, with a focus growing decan, the Greek system of global Gods, indication rulership.

The risings of the decans in the evening were used to separate the night into 'hrs.' The rising of a constellation before daybreak (its heliacal increase) was considered the last hr of the evening. Messages from the second century BC listing forecasts relating to the placements of the Earth in zodiac signs during the rising of specific decans, specifically Sothis. The earliest Zodiac found in Egypt days to the first century BC, the Dendera Zodiac.

Particularly essential in the advancement of horoscopic astrology was the astrologer and also astronomer Ptolemy, who resided in Alexandria in Egypt. Ptolemy's job the Tetrabiblos laid the basis of the Western astrological tradition. A resource of next recommendation is said to have "taken pleasure in almost the authority of a Bible amongst the astrological writers of a thousand years or more." It was one of the initial astrological messages to be flowed in the Middle ages Europe after being equated from Arabic right into Latin by Plato of Tivoli (Tiburtinus) in Spain, 1138.

The horoscope and astrology were provided early on to an Egyptian pharaoh named Nechepso and his priest Petosiris. The Hermetic texts were additionally put together throughout this duration and Clement of Alexandria, writing in the Roman era, demonstrates the level to which astrologers were expected to know the texts in his description of Egyptian spiritual ceremonies: This is mainly revealed by their spiritual ceremonial. For first developments, the Singer, birthing someone of the symbols of music. For they claim that he must discover two of the books of Hermes, the among which has the hymns of the gods, the second the laws for the king's life. He has to have the astrological books of Hermes, which are four in number, always in his mouth.

Greece and also Rome

Also, Greek influence played a crucial duty in the transmission of astrological concepts to Rome. Nevertheless, our earliest references to demonstrate its arrival in Rome disclose its initial impact upon the reduced orders of culture, and display worry concerning the uncritical choice to the ideas of Babylonian 'star-gazers'. Amongst the Greeks as well as Romans, Babylonia (additionally known as Chaldea) ended up being so understood astrology that 'Chaldean wisdom' became a common basic synonym for divination using worlds and also celebrities.

The initial guaranteed referral to astrology comes from the work of the orator Cato, who, in 160

BC, composed a writing caution farm movie director against consulting with Chaldeans. The 2nd-century Roman poet Juvenal, in his satirical attack on the practices of Roman ladies, likewise complains regarding the prevalent influence of Chaldeans, regardless of their lowly social condition, stating "Still more relied on are the Chaldaeans; every word uttered by the astrologist they will think has actually originated from Hammon's fountain, ... nowadays no astrologist has credit unless he has actually been put behind bars in some distant camp, with chains clanking on either arm".

One of the first astrologists to bring Hermetic astrology to Rome was Thrasyllus, that, in the early century CE, acted as the astrologist for the emperor Tiberius. Tiberius was the first emperor reported having had a court astrologist, although his predecessor Augustus had likewise made use of astrology to legitimize his Imperial legal rights. In the 2nd century CE, the astrologer Claudius Ptolemy was so stressed with obtaining horoscopes precise that he began the first effort to make an exact world map (maps before this were more relativistic or allegorical) to ensure that he might chart the connection in between the individual's birthplace as well as the heavenly bodies. While doing so, he created the term "location."

Even though some use astrology by the emperors shows up to have happened, there was additionally a prohibition on astrology to a particular degree also. In the 1st century, Publius Antonius was implicated in the criminal offense of funding the eliminated astrologist Pammenes and requesting his horoscope and that of after that emperor Nero. For this criminal offense, Nero compelled Anteius to commit self-destruction. At this time, astrology was likely to cause fees of magic and also treason.

Cicero's De divinatione (44 BCE), which rejects astrology and various other presumably divinatory strategies, is a fruitful historical resource for the conception of scientificity in classic Roman Antiquity. The Pyrrhonist thinker Sextus Empiricus assembled the old arguments against astrology in his book Against the Astrologers.

Numerous societies have joined significance to cosmic occasions, and the Indians, Chinese, and Maya created expand frameworks for foreseeing earthbound events from heavenly perceptions. In the West, astrology regularly comprises an arrangement of horoscopes implying to clarify parts of an individual's character and anticipate future incidents throughout their life depends on the places of the sun, moon, and other heavenly articles at the hour of their introduction to the world. Most of the expert celestial prophets depend on such frameworks.

Astrology has been dated to in any event the second thousand years BCE, with establishes in calendrical frameworks used to foresee occasional movements and to decipher heavenly cycles as indications of perfect correspondences. A type of astrology was drilled in the primary administration of Mesopotamia (1950–1651 BCE). Vedāṅga Jyotiṣa is one of the most punctual known Hindu messages on cosmology and astrology (Jyotisha). The content is dated between 1400 BCE to conclusive hundreds of years BCE by different researchers as indicated by cosmic and semantic confirmations. Chinese astrology was expounded in the Zhou administration (1046–256 BCE).

Greek astrology after 332 BCE blended Babylonian astrology in with Egyptian Decanic astrology in Alexandria, making horoscopic astrology. Alexander the Great's victory of Asia permitted astrology to spread to Ancient Greece and Rome.

In Rome, astrology was related to 'Chaldean shrewdness.' After the triumph of Alexandria in the seventh century, astrology was taken up by Islamic researchers, and Hellenistic writings were converted into Arabic and Persian.

In the twelfth century, Arabic scripts were imported to Europe and translated into Latin. Significant space experts, including Tycho Brahe, Johannes Kepler, and Galileo, rehearsed as celestial court prophets. Visionary references show up in writing underway of artists, for example, Dante Alighieri and Geoffrey Chaucer, and of dramatists, for example, Christopher Marlowe and William Shakespeare.

All through the vast majority of its history, astrology was viewed as an insightful custom. It was acknowledged in political and literary settings and was associated with different examinations, for example, space science, speculative chemistry, meteorology, and medication. Toward the finish of the seventeenth century, new logical ideas in space science and material science (for example, heliocentrism and Newtonian mechanics) raised doubt about astrology. Astrology hence lost its scholarly and hypothetical standing, and fundamental faith in astrology has, to a great extent, declined.

Antiquated world

Astrology, in its broadest sense, is the quest for significance in the sky. Early proof for people making cognizant endeavors to quantify, record, and foresee regular changes by reference to galactic cycles, shows up as markings on bones and cavern dividers, which show that lunar cycles were being noted as ahead of schedule as 25,000 years back. This was an initial move towards recording the Moon's impact upon tides and streams, and towards sorting out a shared table. Ranchers tended to agrarian necessities with expanding information on the heavenly bodies that show up in the various seasons—and utilized the ascending of specific star-gatherings to proclaim yearly floods or occasional exercises. By the third thousand years BCE, civilizations had advanced attention to divine cycles and may have arranged sanctuaries in arrangement with heliacal risings of the stars.

Dispersed proof proposes that the most established realized celestial references are duplicates of writings made in the old world. The Venus tablet of Ammisaduqa is believed to be arranged in Babylon around 1700 BCE. A parchment recording an early utilization of electional astrology is dubiously attributed to the rule of the Sumerian ruler Gudea of Lagash (c. 2144 – 2124 BCE).

This portrays how the divine beings uncovered to him in fantasy the heavenly bodies that would be generally ideal for the arranged development of a sanctuary. Nonetheless, there is debate about whether these were really recorded at that point or simply attributed to antiquated rulers by children. The most established indisputable proof of the utilization of astrology as an incorporated arrangement of information is along these lines credited to the records of the principal tradition of Mesopotamia (1950–1651 BCE). This astrology had a few equals with Hellenistic Greek (western) astrology, including the zodiac, a norming points close to 9 degrees in Aries, the trine perspective, planetary praises, and the dodekatemoria (the twelve divisions of 30 degrees each). The Babylonians saw divine occasions as potential signs as opposed to as reasons for physical opportunities.

The arrangement of Chinese astrology was expounded during the Zhou administration (1046–256 BCE) and prospered during the Han Dynasty (second century BCE to second century CE), during which all the commonplace components of conventional Chinese culture – the Yin-Yang reasoning, hypothesis of the five elements, Heaven and Earth, Confucian ethical quality – were united in formalizing the philosophical standards of Chinese medication and divination, astrology and speculative chemistry.

Old protests

Cicero expressed the twins' complaint (that with close birth times, individual results can be altogether different), later created by Saint Augustine. He contended that since different planets are significantly more removed from the earth than the moon, they could have, without a doubt, minor impact contrasted with the satellites. He additionally contended that on the off chance that astrology clarifies everything about an individual's destiny, at that point, it wrongly disregards the noticeable impact of acquired capacity and child-rearing, changes in wellbeing worked by medication or the effects of the climate on individuals.

Plotinus contended that since the fixed stars are substantially more far off than the planets, it is funny to envision the planets' impact on human undertakings ought to rely upon their situation as for the zodiac. He additionally contends that the translation of the moon's combination with a planet as significant when the moon is full, however awful when the moon is winding down, is off-base, as, from the moon's perspective, half of its surface is consistently in daylight. From the planet's perspective, fading ought to be better, as then the world sees some light from the moon, yet when the moon is full to us, it is dim, and in this manner awful, as an afterthought confronting the planet being referred to.

Favorinus contended that it was ludicrous to envision that stars and planets would influence human bodies similarly as they affect the tides, and equally impossible that little movements in the sky cause considerable changes in individuals' destinies. Sextus Empiricus contended that it was ludicrous to interface human properties with fantasies about the indications of the zodiac.

Carneades argued that confidence in the future denies free choice and profound quality; that individuals conceived at various occasions would all be able to kick the bucket in a similar mishap or fight, and that in opposition to uniform impacts from the stars, clans, and societies are on the whole unique.

Greek Egypt

In 525 BCE, Egypt was conquered by the Persians. The first century BCE Egyptian Dendera Zodiac shares two signs – the Balance and the Scorpion – with Mesopotamian astrology.

With the occupation by Alexander the Great in 332 BCE, Egypt got Hellenistic. The city of Alexandria was established by Alexander after the triumph, turning into where Babylonian astrology was blended in with Egyptian Decanic astrology to make Horoscopic astrology. This contained the Babylonian zodiac with its arrangement of planetary magnifications, the triplicities of the signs, and the significance of shrouds. It utilized the Egyptian idea of partitioning the constellation into thirty-six decans of ten degrees each, with an accentuation on the rising decan, and the Greek arrangement of planetary Gods, sign rulership and four components.

Second century BCE messages foresee places of planets in zodiac signs at the hour of the ascending of certain decans, especially Sothis. The celestial prophet and stargazer Ptolemy lived in Alexandria. Ptolemy's work, the Tetrabiblos, shaped the premise of Western astrology, and, "...appreciated nearly the authority of a Bible among the visionary essayists of a thousand years or more."

Greece and Rome

The triumph of Asia by Alexander the Great presented the Greeks to thoughts from Syria, Babylon, Persia, and focal Asia. Around 280 BCE, Berossus, a cleric of Bel from Babylon, moved to the Greek island of Kos, showing astrology and Babylonian culture. By the first century BCE, there were two assortments of astrology, one utilizing horoscope to depict the past, present, and future; the other, theurgic, stressing the spirit's rising to the stars. Greek impact assumed a vital job in the transmission of celestial hypothesis to Rome.

The primary unmistakable reference to astrology in Rome originates from the speaker Cato, who in 160 BCE cautioned ranch regulators against counseling with Chaldeans, who were portrayed as Babylonian 'star-gazers'. Among the two Greeks and Romans, Babylonia turned out to be so related to astrology that 'Chaldean astuteness' got synonymous with divination utilizing planets and stars.

The second-century Roman writer and comedian Juvenal gripes about the inescapable impact of Chaldeans, saying, "Still increasingly trusted are the Chaldaeans; each word expressed by the soothsayer they will accept has originated from Hammon's wellspring."

One of the primary crystal gazers to carry Hermetic astrology to Rome was Thrasyllus, stargazer to the sovereign Tiberius, the principal ruler to have had a court celestial prophet. However, his ancestor Augustus had utilized astrology to help legitimize his Imperial rights.

Medieval world

The original writings after that traditional Indian astrology are based are early medieval accumulations, quite the Bṛhat Parāśara Horāśāstra, and Sārāvalī by Kalyāṇavarma. The Horāshastra is a composite work of 71 sections, of which the initial segment (chapters 1–51) dates to the seventh to mid-eighth hundreds of years and the subsequent part (chapters 52–71) to the later eighth century. The Sārāvalī in like manner dates to around 800 CE.[49] English interpretations of these writings were distributed by N.N. Krishna Rau and V.B. Choudhari in 1963 and 1961, individually.

Islamic

Astrology was taken up by Islamic researchers following the breakdown of Alexandria to the Arabs in the seventh century and the establishment of the Abbasid domain in the eighth. The second Abbasid caliph, Al Mansur (754–775) built the city of Baghdad to go about as a focal point of learning and remembered for its plan a library-interpretation focus known as Bayt al-Hikma 'Place of Wisdom,' which kept on getting advancement from his beneficiaries and was to give a significant stimulus to Arabic-Persian interpretations of Hellenistic visionary writings. The early interpreters included Mashallah, who assisted with choosing the ideal opportunity for the establishment of Baghdad, and Sahl ibn Bishr, (a.k.a. Zael), whose writings were legitimately compelling upon later European soothsayers, for example, Guido Bonatti in the thirteenth century, and William Lilly in the seventeenth century. Information on Arabic writings began to get brought into Europe during the Latin interpretations of the twelfth century.

Europe

The first visionary book distributed in Europe was the Liber Planet is et Mundi Climatibus ("Book of the Planets and Regions of the World"), which showed up somewhere in the range of 1010 and 1027 AD. Gerbert of Aurillac may have composed it. Ptolemy's second century AD Tetrabiblos was converted into Latin by Plato of Tivoli in 1138. The Dominican scholar Thomas Aquinas followed Aristotle in recommending that the stars administered the flawed 'sublunary' body while endeavoring to accommodate astrology with Christianity by expressing that God controlled the spirit. The thirteenth-century mathematician Campanus of Novara is said to have conceived an arrangement of visionary houses that partitions the prime vertical into 'places' of equivalent 30° curves; however, the framework was utilized before in the East. The thirteenth-century stargazer Guido

Bonatti composed a coursebook, the Liber Astronomicus, a duplicate of which King Henry VII of England claimed toward the finish of the fifteenth century.

In Paradiso, the last piece of the Divine Comedy, the Italian writer Dante Alighieri alluded "in incalculable subtleties" to the mysterious planets, however, he adjusted conventional astrology to suit his Christian perspective, for instance, utilizing celestial speculation in his predictions of the change of Christendom.

Medieval protests

In the seventh century, Isidore of Seville contended in his Etymologiae that stargazing portrayed the developments of the sky. At the same time, astrology had two sections: one was logical, depicting the events of the sun, the moon, and the stars, while the other, making expectations, was religiously mistaken. Interestingly, John Gower, in the fourteenth century, characterized astrology as basically constrained to the creation of expectations. The impact of the stars was thus separated into traditional astrology, with, for instance, consequences for tides and the development of plants, and legal astrology, with apparently unsurprising implications for individuals.

The fourteenth-century doubter Nicole Oresme anyway remembered cosmology as a piece of astrology for his Livre de divinations. Oresme contended that present ways to deal with the forecast of occasions, for example, torment, wars, and climate, were improper, yet that such expectation was a substantial field of the request. Be that as it may, he assaulted the utilization of astrology to pick the planning of activities (purported cross-examination and political decision) as entirely bogus. He dismissed the assurance of human action by the stars on the grounds of through and through freedom.

The monk Laurens Pignon (c. 1368–1449) comparatively rejected all types of divination and determinism, including by the stars, in his 1411 Contre fewer Devineurs. This was contrary to the convention conveyed by the Arab cosmologist Albumasar (787-886), whose Introductorium in Astronomiam and De Magnis Coniunctionibus contended the view that the stars control both individual activities and more prominent scope history.

In the late 1400s, Giovanni Pico Della Mirandola vigorously assaulted astrology in Disputationes contra Astrologos, contending that the sky neither caused, nor proclaimed natural occasions. His contemporary, Pietro Pomponazzi, a "rationalistic and basic mastermind," was substantially more optimistic about astrology and condemning of Pico's assault.

Renaissance and Early Modern

Renaissance researchers generally rehearsed astrology. Gerolamo Cardano cast the horoscope of Lord Edward VI of England, while John Dee was the individual stargazer to sovereign Elizabeth I of England. Catherine de Medici paid Michael Nostradamus in 1566 to confirm the forecast of the passing of her better half, ruler Henry II of France, made by her stargazer Lucus Gauricus. Significant space experts who rehearsed as celestial court prophets included Tycho Brahe in the imperial court of Denmark, Johannes Kepler to the Habsburgs, Galileo Galilei to the Medici, and Giordano Bruno who was singed at stake for apostasy in Rome in 1600. The differentiation among astrology and cosmology was not so much clear. Advances in space science were frequently propelled by the craving to improve the exactness of astrology.

Ephemerides with complex prophetic figurings, and chronological registries deciphering heavenly occasions for use in medication and for picking times to plant crops, were well known in Elizabethan England. In 1597, the English mathematician and doctor Thomas Hood made a lot of paper instruments that utilized spinning overlays to assist understudies with working out connections between fixed stars or heavenly bodies, the midheaven, and the twelve celestial houses. The planets and signs administered hood's instruments likewise outlined, for educational purposes, the alleged connections between the indications of the zodiac, the worlds, and the pieces of the human body disciples accepted. While Hood's introduction was creative, his mysterious data was generally standard and was taken from Gerard Mercator's prophetic circle made in 1551, or a source utilized by Mercator.

English astrology had arrived at its pinnacle by the seventeenth century. Stargazers were scholars, scientists, and social architects, just as giving individuals appeal to everybody from rulers downwards. In addition to other things, crystal gazers professed to have the option to prompt on the best time to take an excursion or reap a harvest, analyze and recommend for physical or psychological maladjustments, and foresee catastrophic events. This supported a framework where everything — individuals, the world, the universe — was comprehended to be interconnected, and astrology existed together cheerfully with religion, enchantment, and science.

Illumination period and onwards

During the Enlightenment, scholarly compassion toward astrology fell away, leaving just a well-known after upheld by modest chronological registries. One English chronicle compiler, Richard Saunders, followed the soul of the age by printing a scornful Discourse on the Invalidity of Astrology, while in France Pierre Bayle's Dictionnaire of 1697 expressed that the subject was immature. The Anglo-Irish humorist Jonathan Swift derided the Whig political crystal gazer, John Partridge.

Astrology saw a well-known restoration beginning in the nineteenth century, as a feature of a general recovery of mysticism and—later, New Age reasoning, and through the impact of broad communications, for example, paper horoscopes. From the get-go in the twentieth century, the specialist Carl Jung built up specific ideas concerning astrology, which prompted the improvement of mental astrology.

Standards and Practice of Astrology

Promoters have characterized astrology as a symbolic language, and artistic expression, a science, and a technique for divination. Although most mundane astrology frameworks share regular roots in old ways of thinking that affected one another, many useful techniques that contrast from those in the West. These incorporate Hindu astrology (otherwise called "Indian astrology" and in present-day times alluded to as "Vedic astrology") and Chinese astrology, the two of which have impacted the world's social history.

Western

Western astrology is a type of divination dependent on the development of a horoscope for a careful minute, for example, an individual's introduction to the world. It utilizes the tropical zodiac, which is adjusted to the equinoctial focuses.

Western astrology is established on the developments and relative places of heavenly bodies, for example, the Sun, Moon, and planets, which are examined by their development through indications of the zodiac (twelve spatial divisions of the ecliptic) and by their viewpoints (in light of geometric edges) comparative with each other. They are additionally considered by their position in houses (twelve spatial divisions of the sky). Astrology's cutting-edge portrayal in well-known western media is usually decreased to sun sign astrology, which considers just the zodiac indication of the Sun at a person's date of birth, and speaks to only 1/12 of the all-out diagram.

The horoscope outwardly communicates the arrangement of connections for the time and spot of the picked occasion. These connections are between the seven 'planets,' connoting inclinations, for example, war and love, the twelve indications of the zodiac, and the twelve houses. Every planet is in a specific sign and a particular home at the picked time, when seen from a particular place, making two sorts of relationships.

A third kind is the part of every planet to each other world, where for instance, two planets 120° separated (in 'trine') are in an amicable relationship. Yet, two planets 90° separated ('square') are in a tangled relationship. Together these connections and their understandings probably structure "...the language of the sky addressing learned men."

Alongside tarot divination, astrology is one of the center investigations of Western obscurity, and all things considered, has affected frameworks of otherworldly conviction among Western esotericists and Hermeticists, yet besides conviction frameworks, for example, Wicca that have obtained from or been impacted by the Elusive Western convention.

Tanya Luhrmann has said that "all performers know something about astrology." She alludes to a table of correspondences in Starhawk's The Spiral Dance, sorted out via planet, for instance, of the mysterious legend concentrated by entertainers.

The most punctual Vedic content on cosmology is the Vedanga Jyotisha; Vedic idea later came to incorporate astrology too.

Hindu natal astrology started with Hellenistic astrology by the third century BCE,[96]:361[97], however fusing the Hindu lunar houses. The names of the signs (for example Greek 'Krios' for Aries, Hindi 'Kriya'), the planets (for example Greek 'Helios' for Sun, mysterious Hindi 'Heli'), and visionary terms (for example Greek 'apoklima' and 'synapse' for declination and planetary combination, Hindi 'apoklima' and 'sunapha' individually) in Varaha Mihira's writings are viewed as definitive proof of a Greek cause for Hindu astrology.

The Indian methods may likewise have been enlarged with a portion of the Babylonian systems.

Chinese and East Asian

Chinese astrology has a nearby connection with the Chinese way of thinking (hypothesis of the three harmonies: paradise, earth, and man). It uses ideas, for example, yin and yang, the Five stages, the 10 Celestial stems, the 12 Earthly Branches, and Chichen.

The first utilization of Chinese astrology was principally kept to political astrology, the perception of unordinary marvels, an ID of omens, and the determination of auspicious days for occasions and choices.

The star groupings of the Zodiac of western Asia and Europe were not utilized; somewhat, the sky is isolated into Three Enclosures, and Twenty-Eight Mansions in twelve Ci. The Chinese zodiac of twelve creature signs is said to speak to twelve unique kinds of characters. It depends on patterns of years, lunar months, and two-hour times of the day (the chicken).

The zodiac customarily starts with the indication of the Rat, and the cycle continues through 11 different creatures' signs: The Ox, Tiger, Rabbit, Dragon, Snake, Horse, Goat, Monkey, Rooster, Dog, and Pig. Complex frameworks of anticipating destiny and predetermination dependent on one's birthday, birth season, and birth hours, for example, zipping and Zi Wei Dou Shu, are as yet utilized usually in cutting edge Chinese astrology.

They don't depend on direct perceptions of the stars.

The Korean zodiac is indistinguishable from the Chinese one. The Vietnamese planet is practically invisible from the Chinese zodiac aside from the subsequent creature is the Water Buffalo rather than the Ox, and the fourth creature is the Cat rather than the Rabbit. The Japanese have since 1873 commended the start of the new year on 1 January according to the Gregorian schedule.

The Thai zodiac starts, not at Chinese New Year, however either on the first day of the fifth month in the Thai lunar calendar or during the Songkran celebration (presently praised each 13–15 April), contingent upon the motivation behind the utilization.

Philosophical Perspectives: Ancient

St. Augustine (354–430) accepted that the determinism of astrology clashed with the Christian principles of man's choice and obligation, and God not being the reason for malicious. However, he likewise grounded his resistance insightfully, referring to the disappointment of astrology to clarify twins who carry on contrastingly although considered at a similar minute and conceived at around the same time.

Medieval

A portion of the acts of astrology was challenged on religious grounds by medieval Muslim space experts, for example, Al-Farabi (Alpharabius), Ibn al-Haytham (Alhazen), and Avicenna. They said that the strategies for crystal gazers clashed with customary strict perspectives on Islamic researchers, by recommending that the Will of God can be known and anticipated ahead of time. For instance, Avicenna's 'Invalidation against astrology,' Risāla fī ibṭāl aḥkām al-nojūm, contends against the act of astrology while supporting the rule that planets may go about as specialists of perfect causation. Avicenna thought that the development of the worlds impacted life on earth in a deterministic manner, yet contended against the chance of deciding the specific impact of the stars. Avicenna didn't prevent the center authoritative opinion from claiming astrology, yet denied our capacity to comprehend it to the degree that exact and fatalistic forecasts could be produced using it.

Ibn Qayyim Al-Jawziyya (1292–1350), in his Miftah Dar al-SaCadah, likewise utilized physical contentions in space science to scrutinize the act of legal astrology. He perceived that the stars are a lot bigger than the planets, and contended:

Furthermore, if your crystal gazers answer that it is precisely a result of this separation and littleness that their persuasions are immaterial, at that point, how can it be that you guarantee an incredible impact for the littlest superb body, Mercury? Can any anyone explain why you have given an effect to al-Qa's and al-Dhanab, which are two nonexistent focuses

Maimonides, the overwhelming Jewish scholar, space expert, and lawful codifier, composed that astrology is illegal by Jewish law.

Present-day

The Catechism of the Catholic Church keeps up that divination, including prescient astrology, is contrary with present-day Catholic convictions, for example, free choice:

All types of prophecy are to be dismissed: the plan of action to Satan or evil presences, conjuring up the dead or different practices erroneously expected to "reveal" what's to come. Counseling horoscopes, astrology, palm perusing, translation of signs and parts, the wonders of unique insight, and plan of action to mediums all disguise a longing for control after some time, history, and, in the last examination, other people, just as a desire to mollify shrouded powers. They repudiate the respect, regard, and adoring apprehension that we owe to God alone.

Logical Investigation and Analysis

Established researchers reject astrology as having no coherent force for portraying the universe, and thinks of it as a pseudoscience. Consistent testing of astrology has been led, and no proof has been found to help any of the premises or implied impacts sketched out in mysterious conventions.

There is no proposed system of activity by which the positions and movements of stars and planets could influence individuals and occasions on Earth that doesn't repudiate surely knew, fundamental parts of science and physics.[8]:249;[9] Those who keep on having confidence in astrology have been described as doing as such "...in hate of the way that there is no checked logical reason for their convictions, and for sure that there is solid proof in actuality."

Affirmation predisposition is a type of subjective inclination, a mental factor that adds to confidence in astrology. Astrology adherents will, in general, correctly recollect forecasts that end up being valid, and don't recall those that turn out bogus. Another discrete type of affirmation predisposition likewise assumes a job, where adherents frequently neglect to recognize messages that show extraordinary capacity and those that don't. Accordingly, there are two distinct types of affirmation predispositions that are under investigation concerning ideological conviction.

Division

Under the model of falsifiability, first proposed by the scholar of science Karl Popper, astrology is a pseudoscience. Popper viewed astrology as "pseudo-exact" in that "it offers to perception and analysis," yet "by the by doesn't come up to logical guidelines." rather than logical controls, astrology has not reacted to deterioration through the test.

As opposed to Popper, the thinker Thomas Kuhn contended that it was not the absence of falsifiability that makes astrology informal but instead that the procedure and ideas of astrology are non-exact. Kuhn imagined that however celestial prophets had, generally, made expectations that ultimately fizzled, this in itself doesn't make astrology informal, nor do endeavors by crystal gazers to clarify away disappointments by asserting that creating a horoscope is exceptionally troublesome. Or maybe, in Kuhn's eyes, astrology isn't science since it was in every case increasingly much the same as medieval medication; celestial prophets kept a succession of rules and rules for a vital field with known weaknesses.

However, they did not examine because the areas are not manageable to inquire about, thus "they had no riddles to fathom and consequently no science to practice."While a cosmologist could address for disappointment, a celestial prophet proved unable. A stargazer could just clarify away frustration yet couldn't change the visionary theory in a significant manner. In that capacity, to Kuhn, regardless of whether the stars could impact the way people through life, astrology isn't logical.

The logician Paul Thagard affirms that astrology can't be viewed as impaired right now it has been supplanted with a successor. On account of anticipating conduct, brain research is the other option. To Thagard, a further paradigm of the boundary of science from pseudoscience is that the best in class must advance and that the network of specialists ought to endeavor to contrast the present hypothesis with options, and not be "specific in thinking about affirmations and disconfirmations."Progress is characterized here as clarifying new marvels and taking care of existing issues, yet astrology has neglected to advance, having just changed little in almost 2000 years.

To Thagard, celestial prophets are going about only as occupied with ordinary science accepting that the establishments of astrology were entrenched despite the "numerous unsolved issues," and even with better elective speculations (brain research). Consequently, Thagard sees astrology as pseudoscience.

For the thinker Edward W. James, astrology is nonsensical not as a result of the various issues with systems and distortion because of investigations, but since an examination of the prophetic writing shows that it is implanted with misleading rationale and poor thinking.

Imagine a scenario where all through visionary compositions we meet little energy about soundness, unmitigated lack of care toward proof, no feeling of a progressive system of reasons, slight order over the relevant power of criteria, obstinate reluctance to seek after a contention where it leads, unmistakable naivete concerning the viability of clarification, etc. I think we are consummately defended in dismissing astrology as silly. Astrology neglects to fulfill the diverse needs of positive thinking."

Viability

Astrology has not exhibited its feasibility in controlled examinations and has no logical legitimacy. Where it has made falsifiable expectations under controlled conditions, they have been misrepresented. One famous investigation included 28 crystal gazers who were approached to coordinate over a hundred natal diagrams to mental profiles produced by the California Psychological Inventory (CPI) poll.

The twofold visually impaired exploratory convention utilized right now settled upon by a gathering of physicists and a gathering of crystal gazers assigned by the National Council for Geocosmic Research, who advised the experimenters, guaranteed that the test was reasonable and helped draw the focal suggestion of natal astrology to be tried. They additionally picked

26 out of the 28 soothsayers for the tests (two more chipped in a while later).

The examination, distributed in Nature in 1985, found that expectations dependent on natal astrology were no superior to the risk and that the testing "... disproves the visionary theory."

In 1955, the stargazer and analyst Michel Gauquelin expressed that however, he had neglected to discover proof that bolstered markers like zodiacal signs and planetary perspectives in astrology, he found positive relationships between's the daily places of individual planets and accomplishment in callings that astrology customarily connects with those planets.

The most popular of Gauquelin's discoveries depends on the areas of Mars in the natal diagrams of fruitful competitors and got known as the Mars impact. An examination led by seven French researchers endeavored to imitate the case, yet found no factual proof. They ascribed the effect to a specific predisposition on Gauquelin's part, blaming him for trying to convince them to include or erase names from their examination.

Geoffrey Dean has proposed that the impact might be brought about without anyone else announcing of birth dates by guardians instead of any issue with the investigation by Gauquelin. The recommendation is that a little subset of the guardians may have had changed birth times to be predictable with better celestial outlines for a related calling.

The number of births under mysteriously bothersome conditions was additionally lower, showing that guardians pick dates and times to suit their convictions. The example bunch was taken from a period where confidence in astrology was progressively usual. Gauquelin had neglected to discover the Mars impact in later populaces, where a medical attendant or specialist recorded the birth data.

Senior Member, a researcher, and previous stargazer, and clinician Ivan Kelly directed an enormous scope logical test that included more than one hundred subjective, conduct, physical, and different factors—yet found no help for astrology.

Besides, a meta-examination pooled 40 investigations that included 700 crystal gazers and more than 1,000 birth outlines. Ten of the tests—which included 300 members—had the crystal gazers select the correct diagram translation from various others that were not the celestially right graph understanding (usually three to five others). At the point when the date and different evident intimations were evacuated, no critical outcomes proposed there was any favored diagram.

Absence of instruments and consistency

Testing the legitimacy of astrology can be troublesome because there is no agreement among crystal gazers about what astrology is or what it can anticipate. Most expert crystal gazers are paid to foresee the future or depict an individual's character and life; however, most horoscopes just offer ambiguous untestable expressions that can apply to nearly anybody.

Numerous celestial prophets guarantee that astrology is logical, while some have proposed traditional causal specialists, for example, electromagnetism and gravity.

Researchers dismiss these systems as doubtful since, for instance, the attractive field, when estimated from Earth, of a vast yet far off planet, for example, Jupiter is considerably littler than that created by standard family unit apparatuses.

Western astrology has taken the world's pivotal precession (additionally called precession of the equinoxes) into account since Ptolemy's Almagest. Hence, the "main purpose of Aries," the beginning of the celestial year, persistently moves against the foundation of the stars.

The tropical zodiac has no association with the stars, and insofar as no cases are made that the heavenly bodies themselves are in the related sign, celestial prophets keep away from the idea that precession moves the groups of stars.

Charpak and Broch, noticing this, alluded to astrology dependent on the tropical zodiac as being "...empty boxes that have nothing to do with anything and are without any consistency or correspondence with the stars." Sole utilization of the tropical zodiac is conflicting with references made, by similar soothsayers, to the Age of Aquarius, which relies upon when the vernal point enters the heavenly body of Aquarius.

Crystal gazers, for the most part, have just a little information on stargazing and regularly don't consider fundamental standards, for example, the precession of the equinoxes, which changes the situation of the sun with time.

They remarked on the case of Élizabeth Teissier, who asserted that "The sun winds up in a similar spot in the sky on a similar date every year," as the reason for claims that two individuals with a similar birthday, however, many years separated, ought to be under the equivalent planetary impact.

Charpak and Broch noticed that "There is a distinction of around twenty-2,000 miles between Earth's area on a particular date in two progressive years" and that along these lines, they ought not to be under a similar impact as per astrology. Over a 40-year time frame, there would be a distinction more prominent than 780,000 miles.

Astrology and Science

Astrology comprises of various conviction frameworks that hold that there is a connection between galactic wonders and occasions or portrayals of the character in the human world. Established researchers have dismissed astrology as having no illustrative force for portraying the universe. Logical testing has discovered no proof to help the premises or implied impacts plot in prophetic customs.

Where astrology has made falsifiable expectations, it has been misrepresented. The most well-known test was going by Shawn Carlson and incorporated board of researchers and a panel of crystal gazers. It prompted the end that natal astrology played out no superior to risk.

Crystal gazer and analyst Michel Gauquelin professed to have discovered factual help for "the

Mars impact" in the birth dates of competitors, yet it couldn't be duplicated in further examinations. The coordinators of later investigations guaranteed that Gauquelin had attempted to impact their incorporation criteria for the study by recommending explicit people be evacuated. It has additionally been proposed, by Geoffrey Dean, that the revealing of birth times by guardians (before the 1950s) may have caused the evident impact.

Astrology has not exhibited its adequacy in controlled investigations and has no logical legitimacy, and is subsequently viewed as pseudoscience. There is no proposed instrument of activity by which the positions and movements of stars and planets could influence individuals and occasions on Earth in the manner soothsayers state they do that doesn't repudiate surely knew, essential parts of science and material science. Most of the expert celestial prophets depend on performing astrology-based character tests and making pertinent forecasts about the remunerator's future.

The individuals who keep on having confidence in astrology have been described as doing as such "notwithstanding the way that there is no confirmed logical reason for their convictions, and to be sure that there is solid proof unexpectedly." Astrophysicist Neil deGrasse Tyson remarked on ideological conviction, saying, "some portion of realizing how to believe is knowing how the laws of nature shape our general surroundings.

Without that information, without that ability to figure, you can undoubtedly turn into a casualty of individuals who look to exploit you". The establishments of the hypothetical structure utilized in astrology begin with the Babylonians, albeit far-reaching utilization didn't happen till the beginning of the Hellenistic time frame after Alexander the Great moved through Greece.

It was not known to the Babylonians that the groups of stars are not on a heavenly circle and are far separated. The presence of them being close is fanciful. The specific outline of what a star grouping is is social and differed between civilizations. Ptolemy's work on space science was headed somewhat by the craving, similar to always, to figure the planetary developments effectively. Early western astrology worked under the old Greek ideas of the Macrocosm and microcosm. Therefore, clinical astrology related what befell the planets and different items in the sky to clinical tasks. This gave a further help to the investigation of space science. While as yet safeguarding the act of astrology, Ptolemy recognized that the prescient intensity of space science for the movement of the planets and other divine bodies positioned above prophetic expectations.

During the Islamic Golden Age, cosmology was financed with the goal that the galactic parameters, for example, the flightiness of the sun's circle, required for the Ptolemaic model could be determined to a sufficient exactness and accuracy. Those in places of intensity, similar to the Fatimid Caliphate vizier in 1120, subsidized the development of observatories with the goal that mysterious forecasts, fuelled by exact planetary data, could be made. Since the observatories were worked to help in making celestial forecasts, not many of these observatories kept going long because of the denial against astrology inside Islam, and most were torn down during or soon after development.

The away form of astrology in works of cosmology began in 1679, with the yearly production La Connaissance des temps. In contrast to the west, in Iran, the dismissal of heliocentrism proceeded up towards the beginning of the twentieth century, to a limited extent spurred by a dread this would undermine the across the board confidence in astrology and Islamic cosmology in Iran. The principal work, Falak al-Canada by Ictizad al-Saltana, planned for undermining this faith in astrology, and "old cosmology" in Iran was distributed in 1861.

On astrology, it referred to the powerlessness of various soothsayers to make a similar expectation about what happens following combination. It depicted the ascribes stargazers provided for the planets as unrealistic.

Falsifiability

The standard of falsifiability frequently recognizes science and non-science. Logician of science Karl Popper first proposed the basis. To Popper, science doesn't depend on acceptance; instead, logical examinations are characteristically endeavoring to adulterate existing hypotheses through novel tests. On the off chance that a solitary test falls flat, at that point, the theory is diluted.

In this way, any trial of a logical hypothesis must deny specific outcomes that adulterate the theory and expect other explicit issues reliable with the explanation. Utilizing this rule of falsifiability, astrology is a pseudoscience.

Astrology was Popper's most incessant case of pseudoscience. Popper viewed astrology as "pseudo-exact" in that "it offers to perception and trial," yet "in any case doesn't come up to logical measures."

Rather than logical controls, astrology doesn't react to distortion through trial. As indicated by Professor of nervous system science Terence Hines, this is a sign of pseudoscience. "No riddles to settle."

As opposed to Popper, the rationalist Thomas Kuhn contended that it was not the absence of falsifiability that makes astrology informal, but instead that the procedure and ideas of astrology are non-exact.

To Kuhn, although crystal gazers had, verifiably, made expectations that "completely fizzled," this in itself doesn't make it informal, nor do the endeavors by soothsayers to clarify away the disappointment by guaranteeing it was because of the formation of a horoscope being exceptionally troublesome (through subsuming, sometime later, a progressively broad horoscope that prompts an alternate forecast).

Or maybe, in Kuhn's eyes, astrology isn't science since it was in every case increasingly similar to medieval medication; they adhered to a grouping of rules and rules for an essential field with known inadequacies, yet they did no examination because the areas are not manageable to look into, thus, "They had no riddles to explain and hence no science to rehearse."

While a cosmologist could address for disappointment, a celestial prophet proved unable.

A celestial prophet could just clarify away frustration; however, he couldn't reexamine the mysterious speculation in a meaningful manner.

Accordingly, to Kuhn, regardless of whether the stars could impact the way people through life, astrology isn't logical.

Progress, practice, and consistency

Logician Paul Thagard accepted that astrology cannot be viewed as misrepresented right now. It has been supplanted with a successor. On account of anticipating conduct, brain science is the other option. To Thagard, a further measure of the outline of science from pseudoscience was that the best in class must advance and that the network of specialists ought to endeavor to contrast the present hypothesis with choices, and not be "particular in thinking about affirmations and disconfirmations."

Progress is characterized here as clarifying new marvels and taking care of existing issues, yet astrology has neglected to advance, having just changed little in about 2000 years. To Thagard, celestial prophets are going about only as occupied with ordinary science accepting that the establishments of astrology were entrenched despite the "numerous unsolved issues," and notwithstanding better elective hypotheses (Psychology). Therefore, Thagard saw astrology as pseudoscience.

To Thagard, astrology ought not be viewed as a pseudoscience on the disappointment of Gauquelin's to discover any connection between's the different mysterious signs and somebody's vocation, twins not demonstrating the healthy relationships from having similar symptoms in twin examinations, absence of concurrence on the centrality of the planets found since Ptolemy's time and massive scope debacles clearing out people with incomprehensibly various signs simultaneously. Or maybe, his division of science requires three bright foci; "hypothesis, network [and] recorded setting."

While confirmation and falsifiability concentrated on the hypothesis, Kuhn's work centered around the chronicled setting, however, the celestial network ought to likewise be considered. Regardless of whether they:

- Are centered around contrasting their methodology with others.
- Have a steady method.
- Attempt to dilute their hypothesis through analysis.

Right now, distortion, as opposed to adjusting a hypothesis to keep away from the misrepresentation, possibly truly happens when an elective theory is proposed.

Mindlessness

For the thinker Edward W. James, astrology is nonsensical not because of the various issues with instruments and misrepresentation because of examinations, but since an investigation of the prophetic writing shows that it is injected with erroneous rationale and poor thinking.

Consider the possibility that all through celestial compositions we meet little valuation for intelligibility, barefaced lack of care toward proof, no feeling of an order of reasons, slight request over the logical power of criteria, painful reluctance to seek after a contention where it leads, apparent naivete concerning the adequacy of clarification, etc. I think we are superbly advocated in dismissing astrology as unreasonable.

Astrology inherently neglects to satisfy the diverse needs of authentic thinking." This poor thinking incorporates bids to antiquated stargazers, for example, Kepler, regardless of any signs of theme or clear thought, and ambiguous cases. The case that proof for astrology is that individuals conceived at generally "a similar spot have an actual existence design that is fundamentally the same as" is ambiguous, yet additionally overlooks that time is reference outline ward. It gives no meaning of "the same spot" despite the planet's moving in the reference edge of the nearby planetary group. Different remarks by celestial prophets depend on seriously wrong translations of essential material science, for example, a case by one crystal gazer that the nearby planetary group resembles a molecule. Further, James noticed that reaction to analysis additionally depends on the flawed rationale, an example of which was a reaction to twin investigations with the explanation that happenstances in twins are because of astrology, however, any distinctions are because of "heredity and condition," while for different celestial prophets the issues are excessively troublesome.

They simply need to return to their astrology.

Further, to soothsayers, if something shows up in support of them, they lock upon it as verification, while not endeavor to investigate its suggestions, wanting to allude to the thing in favor as conclusive; conceivable outcomes that don't make astrology look ideal are overlooked.

Quinean division

From the Quinean web of information, there is where one should either dismiss astrology or acknowledge astrology yet dismiss all settled logical orders that are contradictory with astrology.

Trial of Astrology

Celestial prophets frequently abstain from making certain expectations and instead depend on dubious articulations that let them attempt to maintain a strategic distance from contamination. Over a few centuries of testing, the expectations of astrology have never been more exact than that normal by chance alone. One methodology utilized in testing astrology quantitatively is through the visually impaired test. At the point when explicit expectations from celestial prophets were tried in thorough test systems in the Carlson test, the forecasts were distorted. Every single controlled investigation has neglected to show any impact.

Carlson's examination

Shawn Carlson's presently famous analysis was performed by 28 crystal gazers coordinating more than 100 natal outlines to mental profiles produced by the California Psychological Inventory (CPI) test utilizing twofold visually impaired strategies.

The exploratory convention utilized in Carlson's examination was consented to by a gathering of physicists and celestial prophets before the test. Divine prophets, selected by the National Council for Geocosmic Research, went about as the mysterious counsels, and assisted with guaranteeing, and concurred, that the test was reasonable. They additionally picked 26 of the 28 crystal gazers for the tests, the other two being intrigued celestial prophets who chipped in a while later. The soothsayers originated from Europe and the United States. The crystal gazers assisted with drawing up the focal recommendation of natal astrology to be tried. Distributed in Nature in 1985, the investigation found that forecasts dependent on natal astrology were no superior to the risk and that the testing "unmistakably invalidates the mysterious theory."

Senior member and Kelly

Researcher and previous crystal gazer Geoffrey Dean and clinician Ivan Kelly directed an enormous scope logical test, including more than one hundred subjective, social, physical, and different factors; however, he found no help for astrology. Further analysis included 45 sure soothsayers, with a normal of 10 years' understanding and 160 guineas pigs (out of a different example size of 1198 guineas pigs) who unequivocally preferred certain qualities in the Eysenck Personality Questionnaire to limits.

The crystal gazers performed a lot of more regrettable than only basing choices off the people's ages, and much more awful than 45 control subjects who didn't utilize birth diagrams by any stretch of the imagination.

Different tests

A meta-investigation was directed, pooling 40 examinations comprising of 700 celestial prophets and more than 1,000 birth outlines. Ten of the tests, which had an aggregate of 300 partaking, included the stargazers choosing the right outline translation from various others that were not the prophetically correct diagram understanding (typically three to five others). At the point when the date and different clear hints were expelled, no critical outcomes were found to recommend there was any favored diagram.

In 10 examinations, members picked horoscopes that they felt were exact portrayals, with one being the "right" answer. Again, the outcomes were no superior to risk. In an investigation of 2011 arrangements of individuals conceived inside 5 minutes of one another ("time twins") to check whether there was any tangible impact, no impact was seen.

Quantitative humanist David Voas analyzed the registration information for over 20 million people in England and Wales to check whether star signs related to marriage game plans. No impact was seen.

Mars impact

In 1955, stargazer and therapist Michel Gauquelin expressed that although he had neglected to discover proof to help such pointers as the zodiacal signs and planetary angles in astrology, he had found positive relationships between's the daily places of a portion of the planets and achievement in callings, (for example, specialists, researchers, competitors, entertainers, scholars, painters, and so forth.), which astrology generally connects with those planets. The most popular of Gauquelin's discoveries depends on the places of Mars in the natal graphs of fruitful competitors and got known as the "Mars impact." An examination led by seven French researchers endeavored to repeat the case, yet found no measurable proof. They credited the impact to particular inclination on Gauquelin's part, blaming him for trying to convince them to include or erase names from their investigation.

Geoffrey Dean has proposed that the impact might be brought about without anyone else detailing of birth dates by guardians as opposed to any issue with the examination by Gauquelin. The proposal is that a little subset of the guardians may have had changed birth times to be reliable with better prophetic graphs for a related calling. The example bunch was taken from a period where faith in astrology was progressively ordinary. Gauquelin had neglected to discover the Mars impact in later populaces, where a medical attendant or specialist recorded the birth data. The number of births under prophetically unwanted conditions was additionally lower, demonstrating more proof that guardians pick dates and times to suit their convictions.

Social effect

In the West, political pioneers have once in a while counseled celestial prophets. For instance, the British knowledge organization MI5 utilized Louis de Wohl as a crystal gazer after cases surfaced that Adolf Hitler employed astrology to time his activities. The War Office was "...interested in comprehending what Hitler's celestial prophets would be letting him know from week to week." truth be told, de Wohl's forecasts were incorrect to the point that he was before long marked a "total imposter," and later proof demonstrated that Hitler considered astrology "complete drivel."

After John Hinckley's endeavored death of US President Ronald Reagan, first woman Nancy Reagan dispatched crystal gazer Joan Quigley to go about as the mystery White House stargazer. Nonetheless, Quigley's job finished in 1988 when it got open through the journals of a former head of staff, Donald Regan.

There was a blast in enthusiasm for astrology in the late 1960s. The humanist Marcello Truzzi portrayed three degrees of association of "Astrology-adherents" to represent its resuscitated ubiquity even with logical ruining.

He found that most astrology-devotees didn't guarantee it was a logical clarification with prescient force. Instead, those externally included, knowing "alongside nothing" about astrology's 'mechanics,' read paper astrology sections, and could profit by "pressure the board of nerves" and "a subjective conviction framework that rises above science."

Those at the subsequent level, for the most part, had their horoscopes thrown and looked for exhortation and forecasts. They were a lot more youthful than those at the primary level. They could profit from information on the language of astrology and the subsequent capacity to have a place with a lucid and select gathering. Those at the third level were exceptionally included and, as a rule, cast horoscopes for themselves.

Astrology gave this little minority of astrology-adherents with an "important perspective on their universe and them a comprehension of their place in it." This third gathering paid attention to astrology, conceivably as a consecrated covering, though the other two collections took it energetically and contemptuously.

In 1953, the humanist Theodor W. Adorno directed an investigation of the astrology segment of a Los Angeles paper as a significant aspect of an undertaking looking at mass culture in industrialist society.

Adorno accepted that mainstream astrology, as a gadget, regularly prompts articulations that energized similarity—and that stargazers who conflict with congruity, by demoralizing execution at work and so on., hazard losing their occupations.

Adorno inferred that astrology is a considerable scope appearance of systematic irrationalism, where people are inconspicuously driven—through honeyed words and dubious speculations—to accept that the creator of the section is tending to them legitimately. Adorno drew a corresponding with the expression opium of the individuals, by Karl Marx, by remarking, "mystery is the metaphysic of the numbskulls."

A 2005 Gallup survey and a 2009 overview by the Pew Research Center announced that 25% of US grown-ups have faith in astrology. As indicated by information discharged in the National Science

Foundation's 2014 Science and Engineering Indicators study, "Fewer Americans dismissed astrology in 2012 than as of late." The NSF study noticed that in 2012, "somewhat the more significant part of Americans said that astrology was 'not under any condition logical,' while almost 66% gave this reaction in 2010. A similar rate has not been this low since 1983."

India and Japan

Birth (in blue) and demise (in red) paces of Japan since 1950, with the abrupt drop in births during hinoeuma year (1966)

In India, there is a since quite a while ago settled and across the board confidence in astrology. It is regularly utilized for day by day life, part especially in issues concerning marriage and profession, and uses electional, horary, and karmic astrology. Indian legislative issues have likewise been impacted by astrology. It is as yet viewed as a part of the Vedanga.

In 2001, Indian researchers and legislators discussed and evaluated a proposition to utilize state cash to subsidize investigation into astrology, bringing about authorization for Indian colleges to offer courses in Vedic astrology.

In February 2011, the Bombay High Court reaffirmed astrology's remaining in India when it rejected a case that tested its status as a science.

In Japan, solid confidence in astrology has prompted emotional changes in the ripeness rate and the number of premature births in the long periods of Fire-Horse.

Disciples accept that ladies conceived in hinoeuma years are unmarriageable and carry misfortune to their dad or spouse. In 1966, the number of infants conceived in Japan dropped by over 25% as guardians attempted to stay away from the shame of having a girl designed in the hinoeuma year.

Writing and music

The fourteenth-century English artists John Gower and Geoffrey Chaucer both alluded to astrology in their works, including Gower's Confessio Amantis and Chaucer's The Canterbury Tales.

Chaucer remarked unequivocally on astrology in his Treatise on the Astrolabe, showing individual information on one territory, legal astrology, with a record of how to locate the ascendant or rising sign.

In the fifteenth century, references to astrology, for example, with likenesses, turned into "an anticipated result" in English writing. The cover sheet of Calderón de la Barca's Astrologo Fingido, Madrid, 1641

In the sixteenth century, John Lyly's 1597 play, The Woman in the Moon, is entirely persuaded by astrology, while Christopher Marlowe makes celestial references in his plays Doctor Faustus and Tamburlaine (both c. 1590), and Sir Philip Sidney alludes to astrology, at any rate, multiple times in his sentiment The Countess of Pembroke's Arcadia (c. 1580).

Edmund Spenser utilizes astrology both beautifully and causally in his verse, uncovering "...unmistakably a standing enthusiasm for the craftsmanship, and intrigue shared by countless his peers." George Chapman's play, Byron's Conspiracy (1608), comparatively utilizes astrology as a causal component in the dramatization. William Shakespeare's demeanor towards astrology is hazy, with conflicting references in plays including King Lear, Antony and Cleopatra, and Richard II.

Shakespeare knew about astrology and utilized his insight into astrology in almost every game he composed, accepting an essential commonality with the subject in his business crowd. Outside theater, the doctor and spiritualist Robert Fludd rehearsed astrology, as did the quack specialist Simon Forman.

In Elizabethan England, "The standard inclination about astrology ... [was] that it is the most valuable of technical disciplines."

In the seventeenth century Spain, Lope de Vega, with a piece of precise information on cosmology, composed plays that scorn astrology. In his peaceful sentiment La Arcadia (1598), it prompts craziness; in his novela Guzman el Bravo (1624), he presumes that the stars were made for man, not man for the stars. Calderón de la Barca composed the 1641 satire Astrologo Fingido (The Pretended Astrologer); the plot was acquired by the French dramatist Thomas Corneille for his 1651 parody Feint Astrologue.

The most well-known bit of music affected by astrology is the symphonic suite The Planets. Composed by the British arranger Gustav Holst (1874–1934), and first acted in 1918, the structure of The Planets depends on the visionary imagery of the planets. Every one of the seven developments of the suite depends on another earth. However, the events are not in the request for the planets from the Sun.

The author Colin Matthews composed an eighth development entitled Pluto, the Renewer, first acted in 2000. In 1937, another British arranger, Constant Lambert, penned an expressive dance on visionary topics, called Horoscope. In 1974, the New Zealand writer Edwin Carr composed The Twelve Signs: An Astrological Entertainment for ensemble without strings. Camille Paglia recognizes astrology as an effect on her work of theoretical analysis Sexual Personae (1990).

CPSIA information can be obtained
at www.ICGtesting.com
Printed in the USA
BVHW090821070521
606415BV00005BA/1557